Regal

Creatures

By Audrey Mac

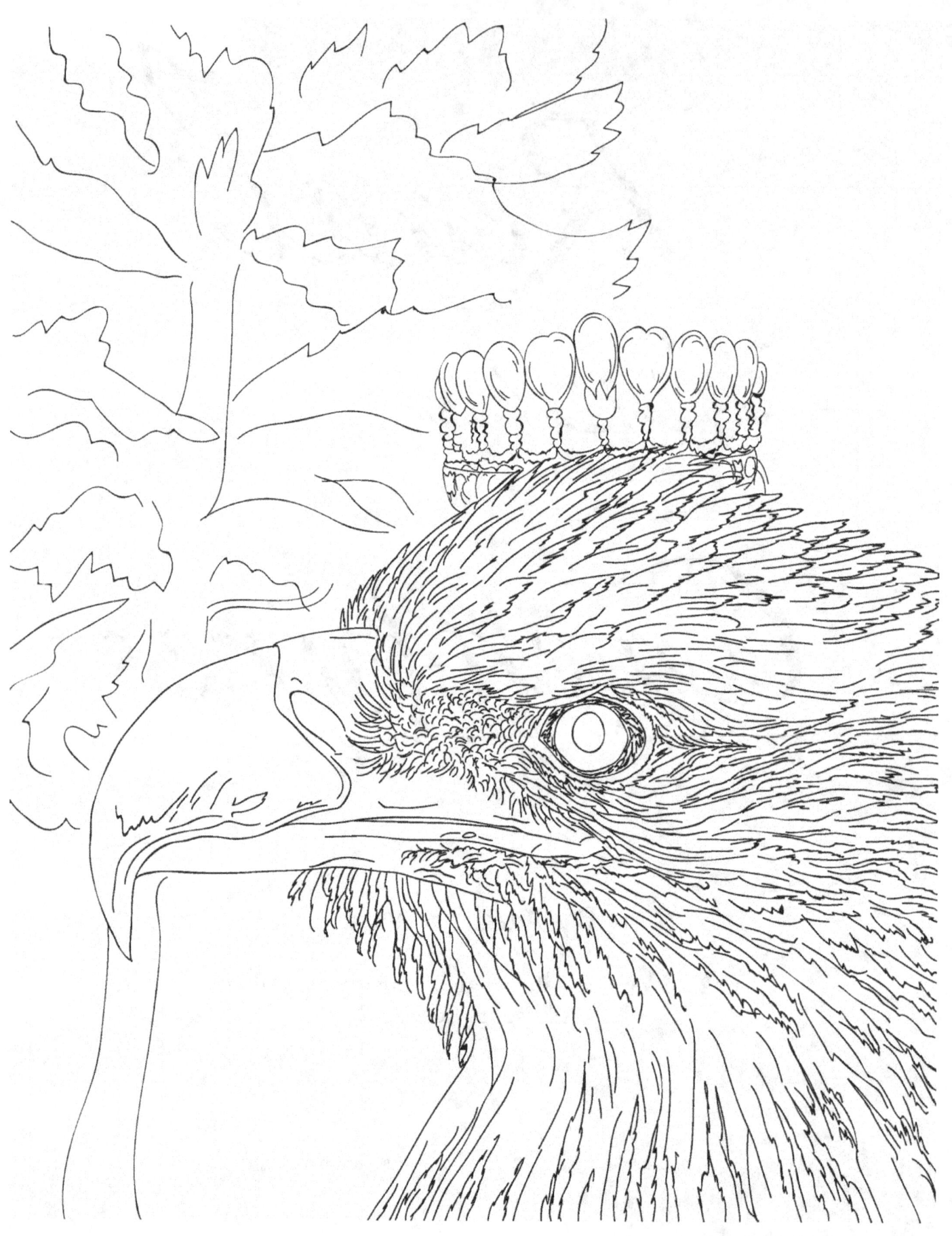

Have you ever wanted to fly like a bird — high in the sky?

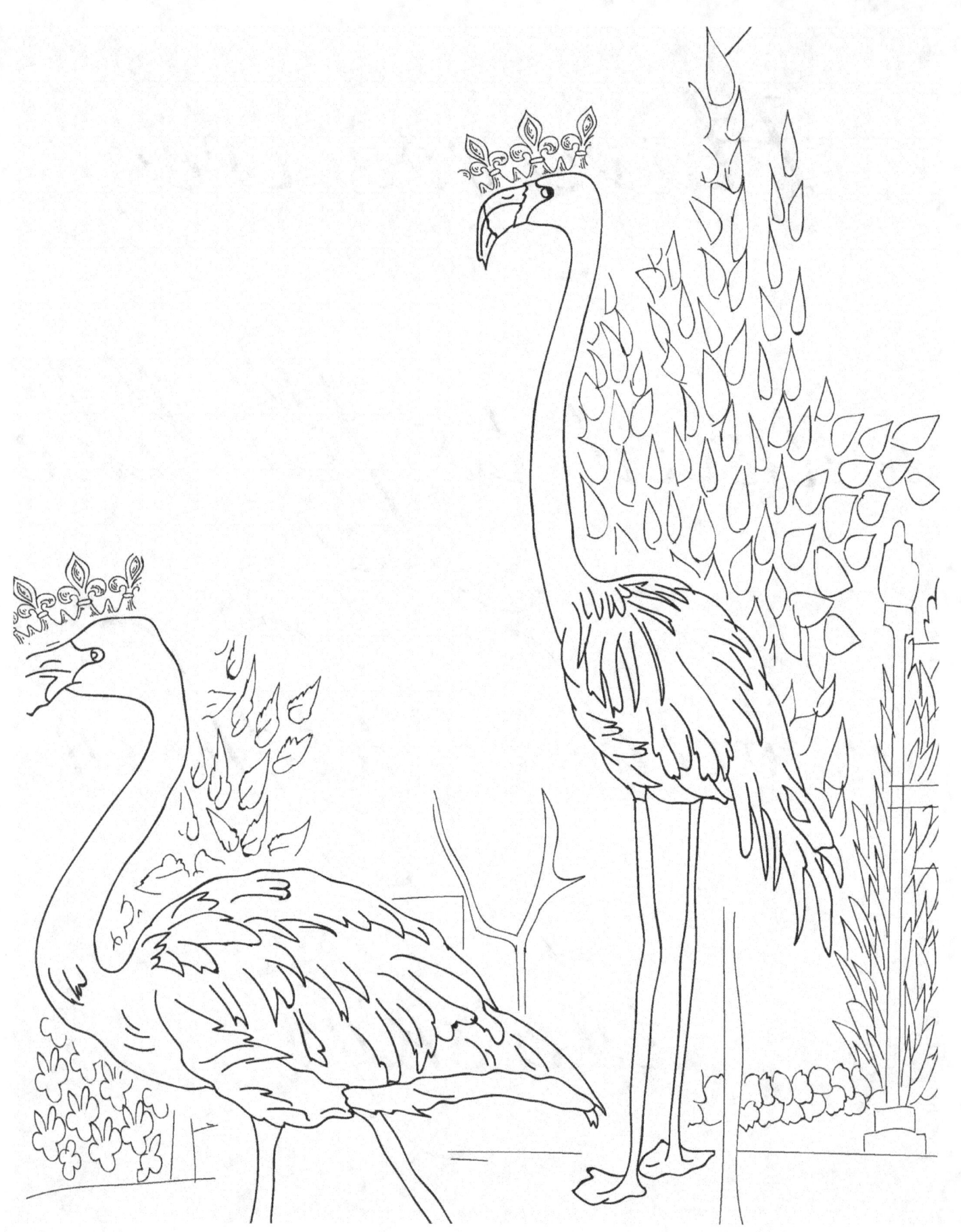

Always hold your
head high and
stand tall — never
look down

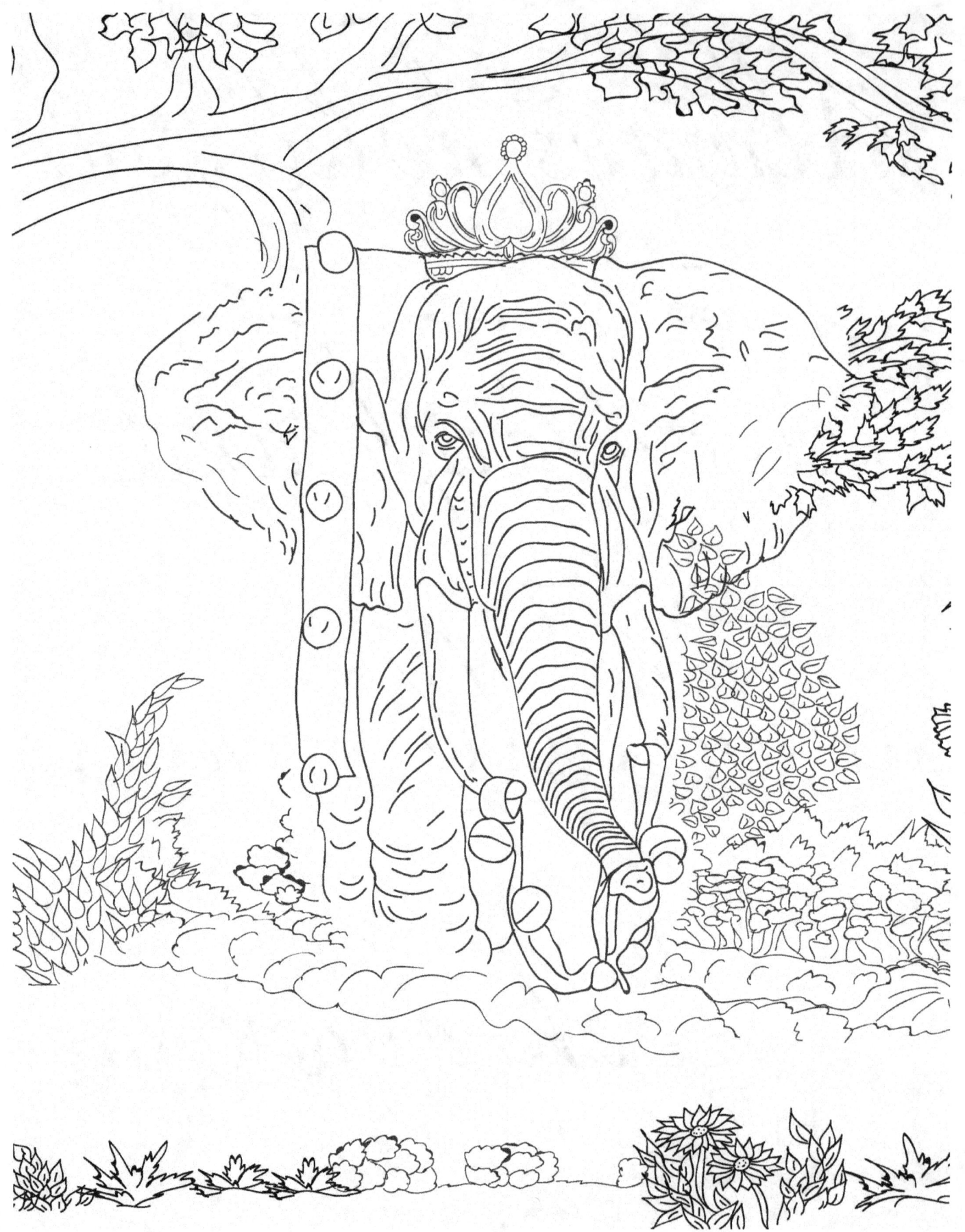

Be strong and
mighty yet gentle
and kind,
always

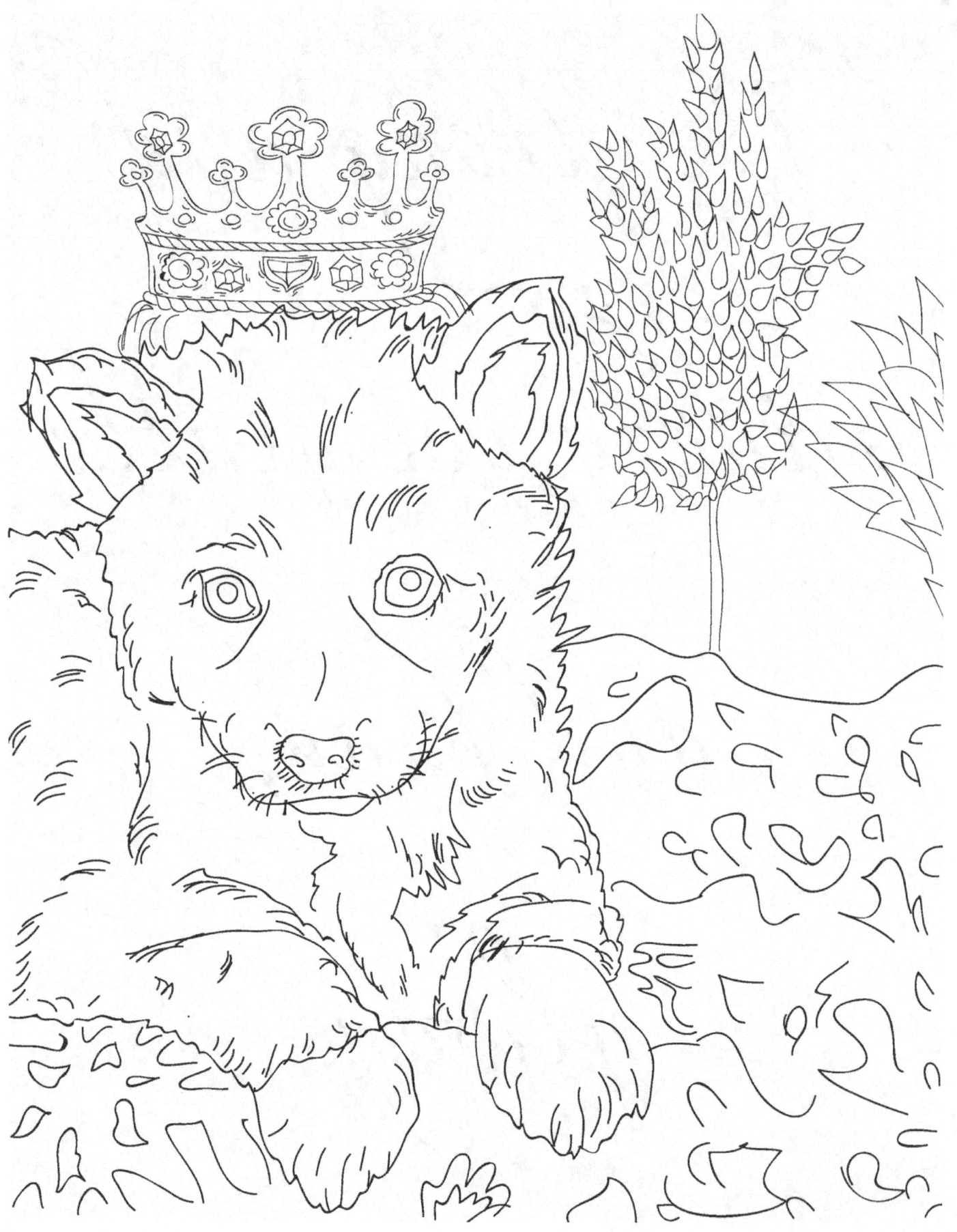

Keep your mind
young with great
imagination
and wonder

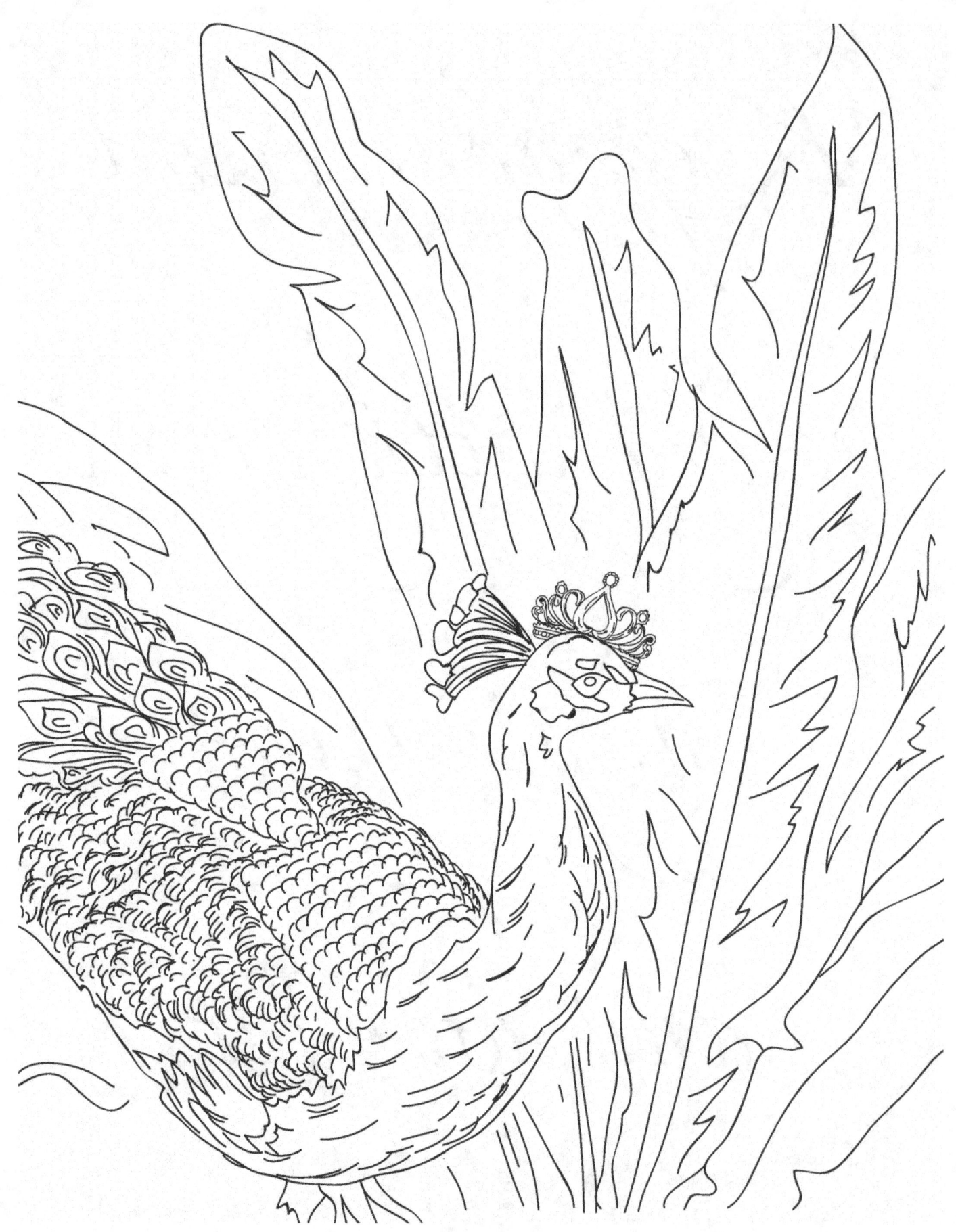

Only show the breadth of your feathers when necessary

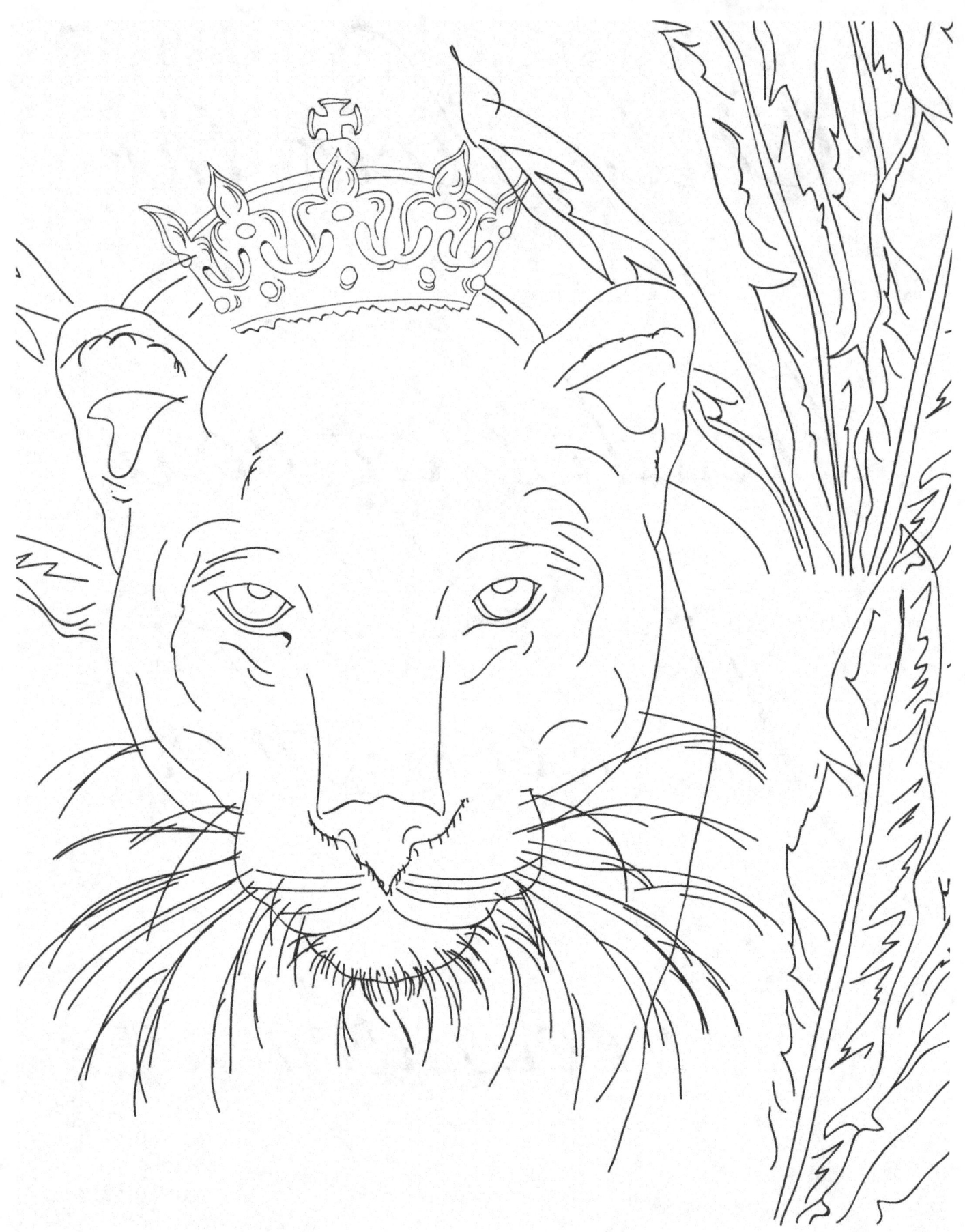

Lurk in the shadows until you are ready to pounce

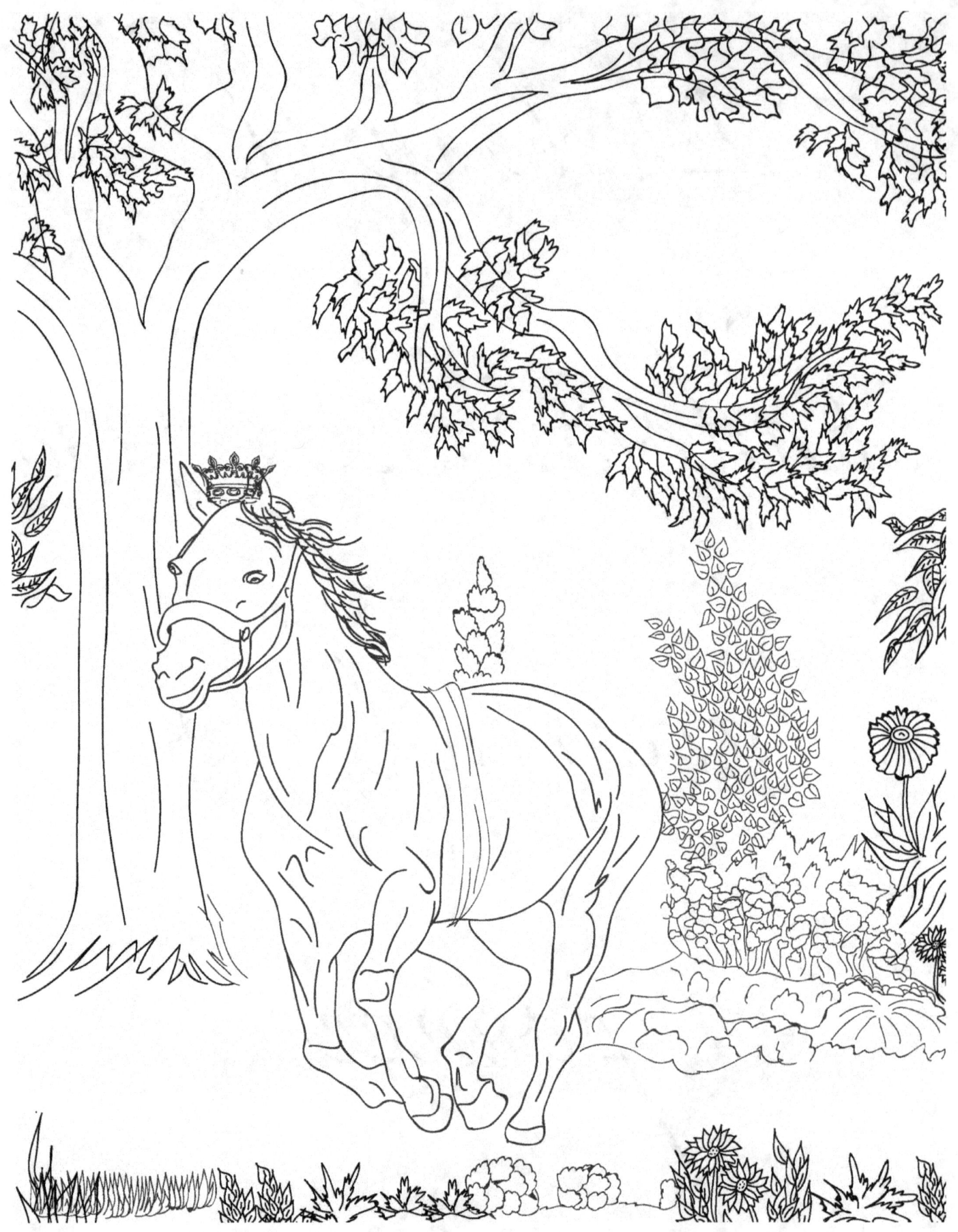

Frolic free always
letting the wind
massage your hair

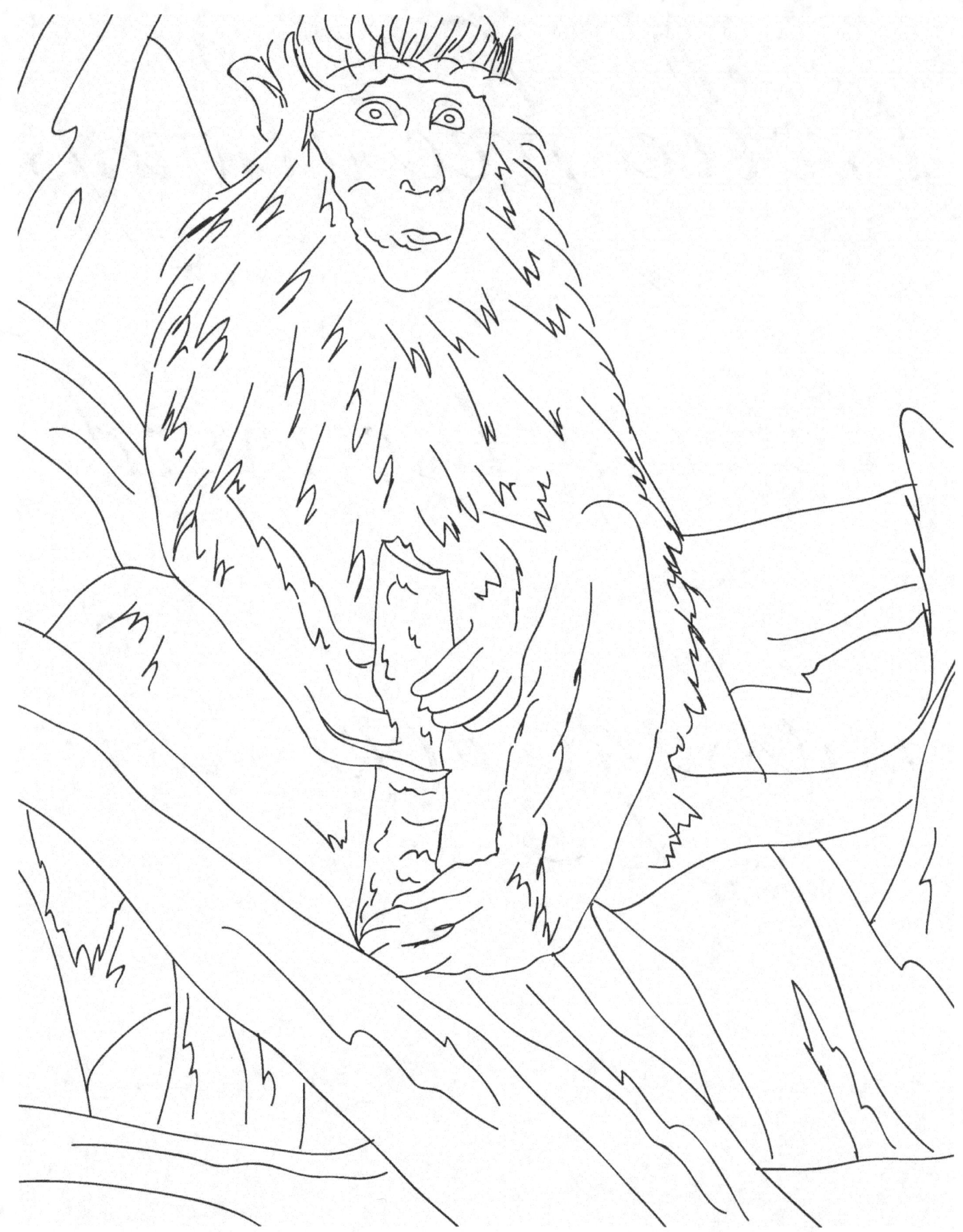

Sometimes you
have to climb a
tree to think alone

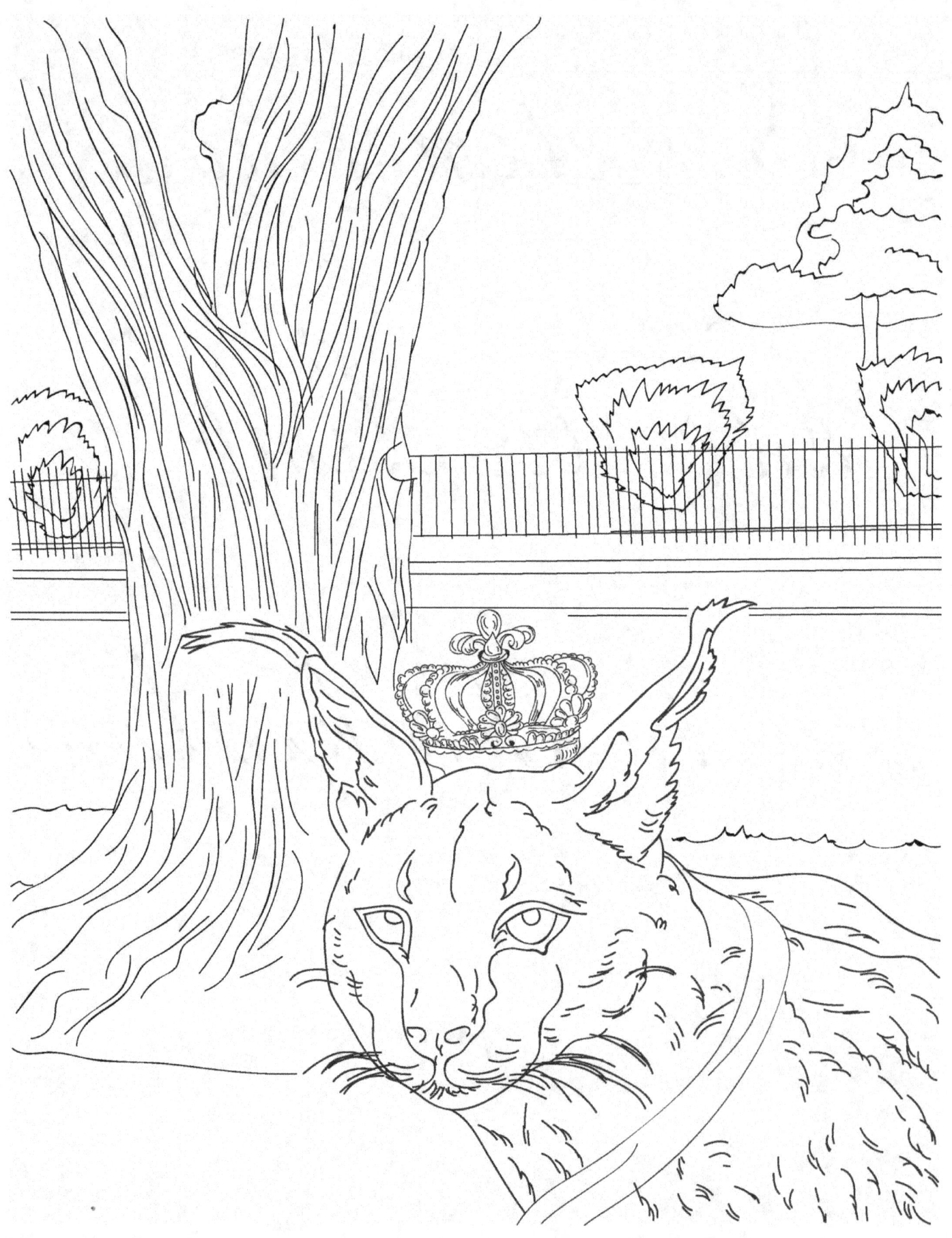

Stay alert in the urban jungle ready to respond on command

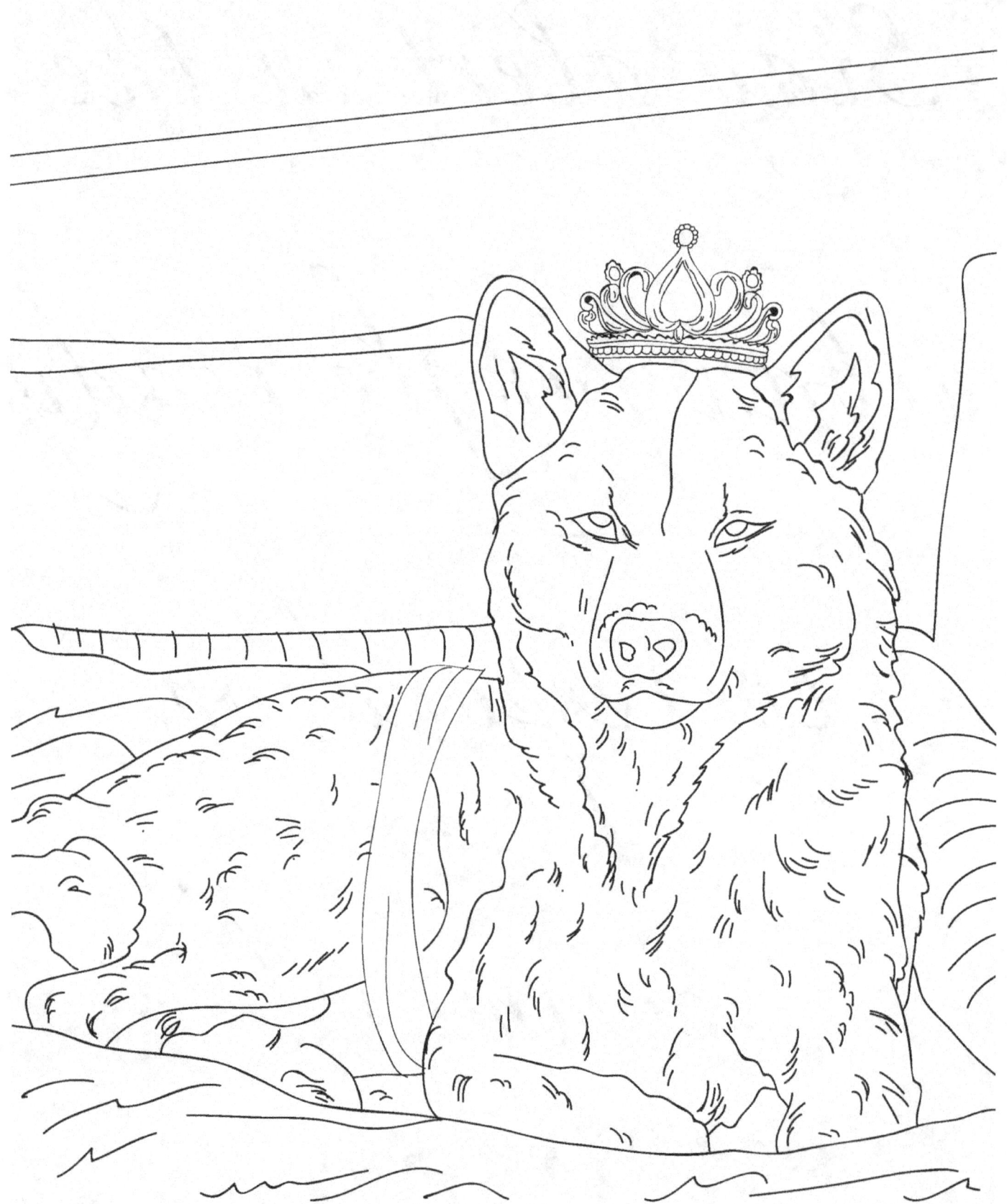

Never forget how regal you are no matter what anyone says

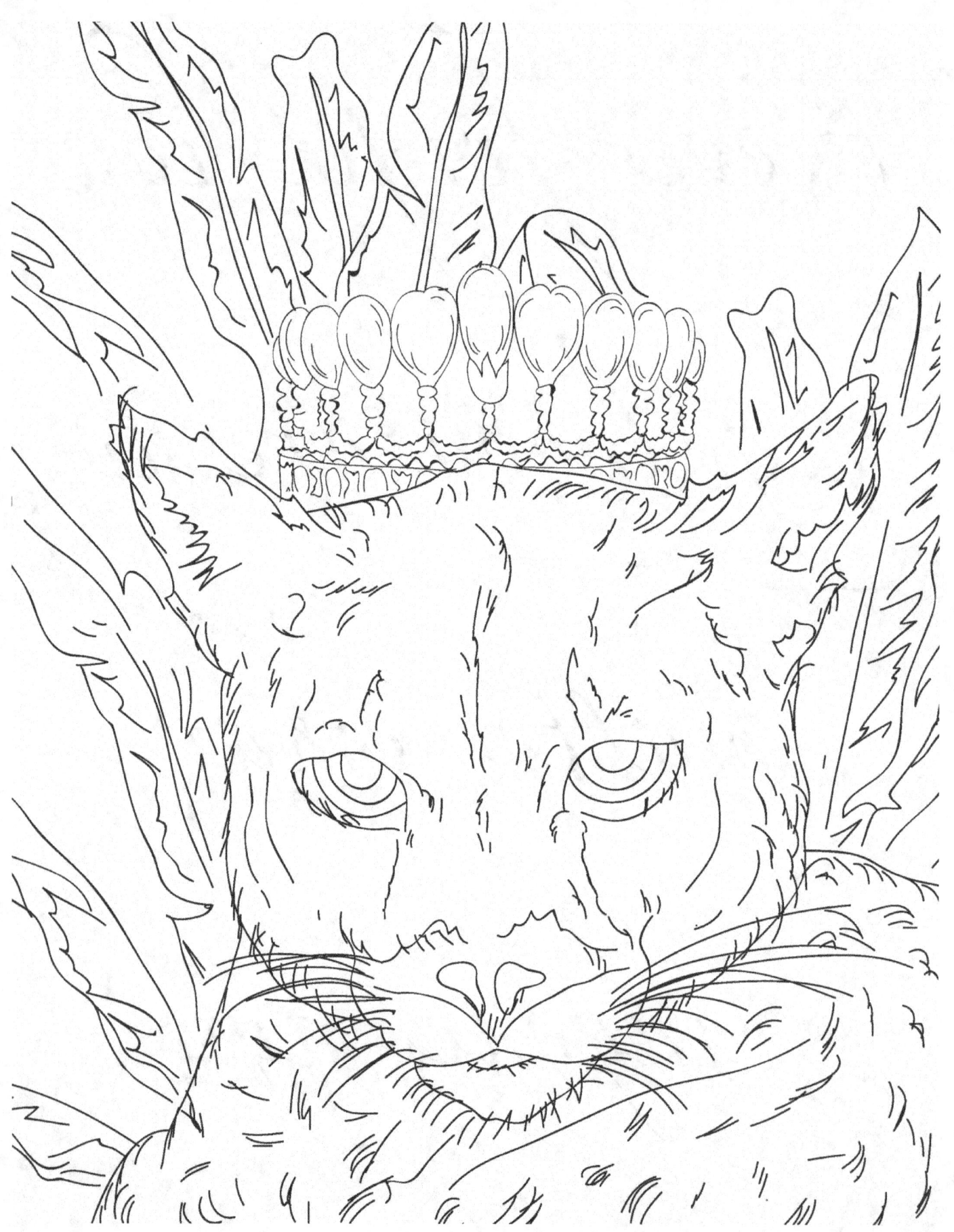

Don't let anyone

borrow your crown

Tell them to get

their own

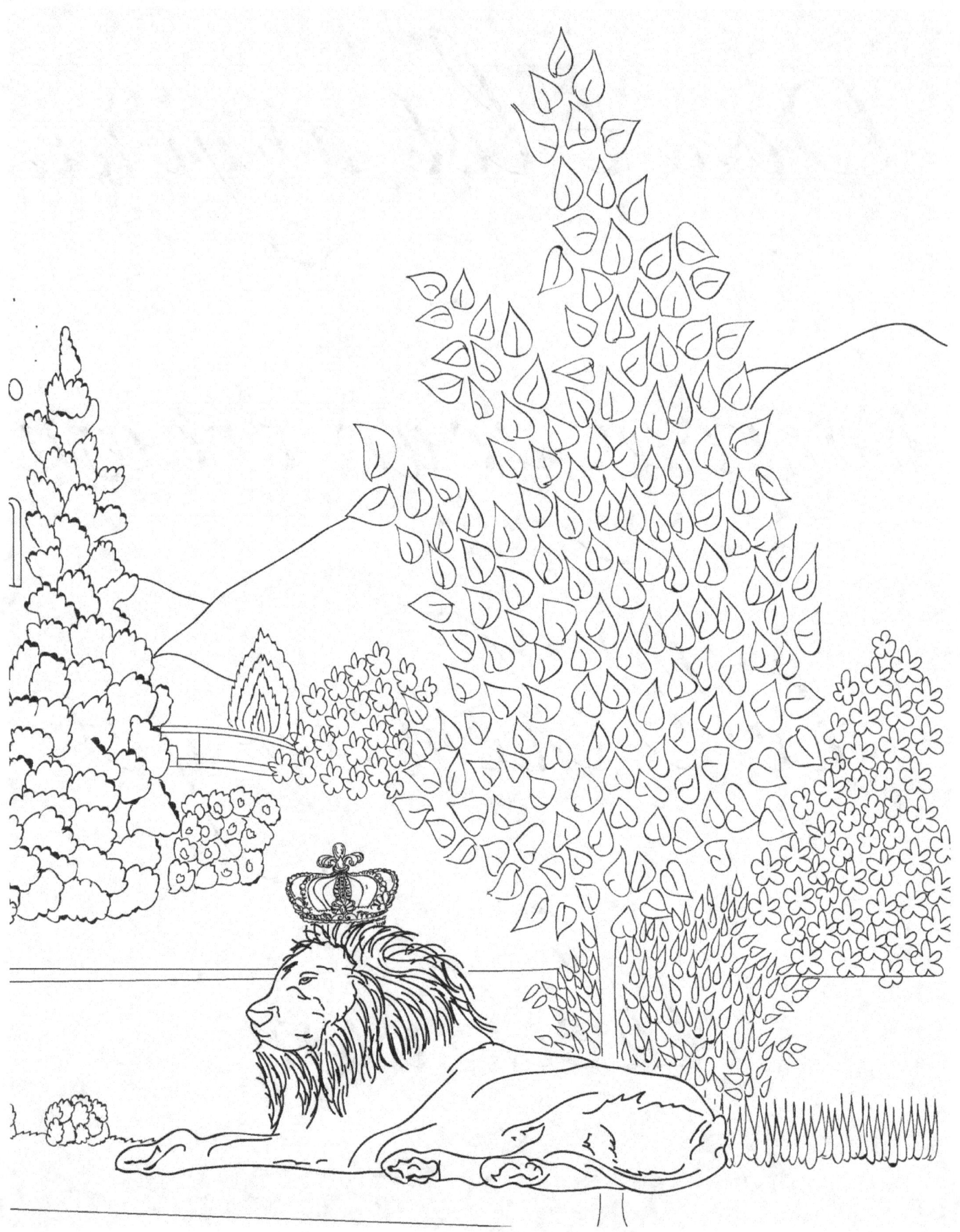

The king is never confused about who's in charge

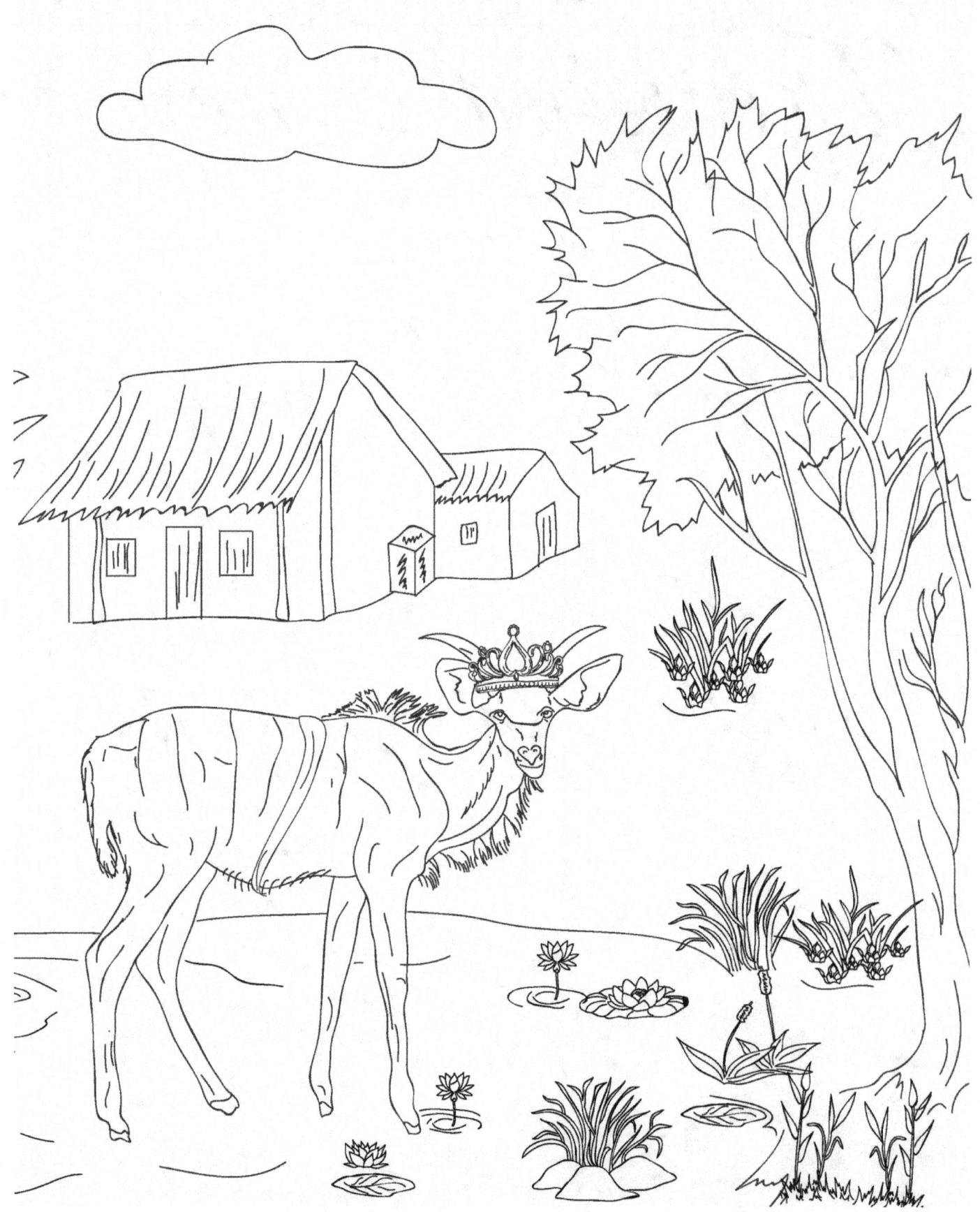

Just be you

wherever you are

no matter what

anyone thinks

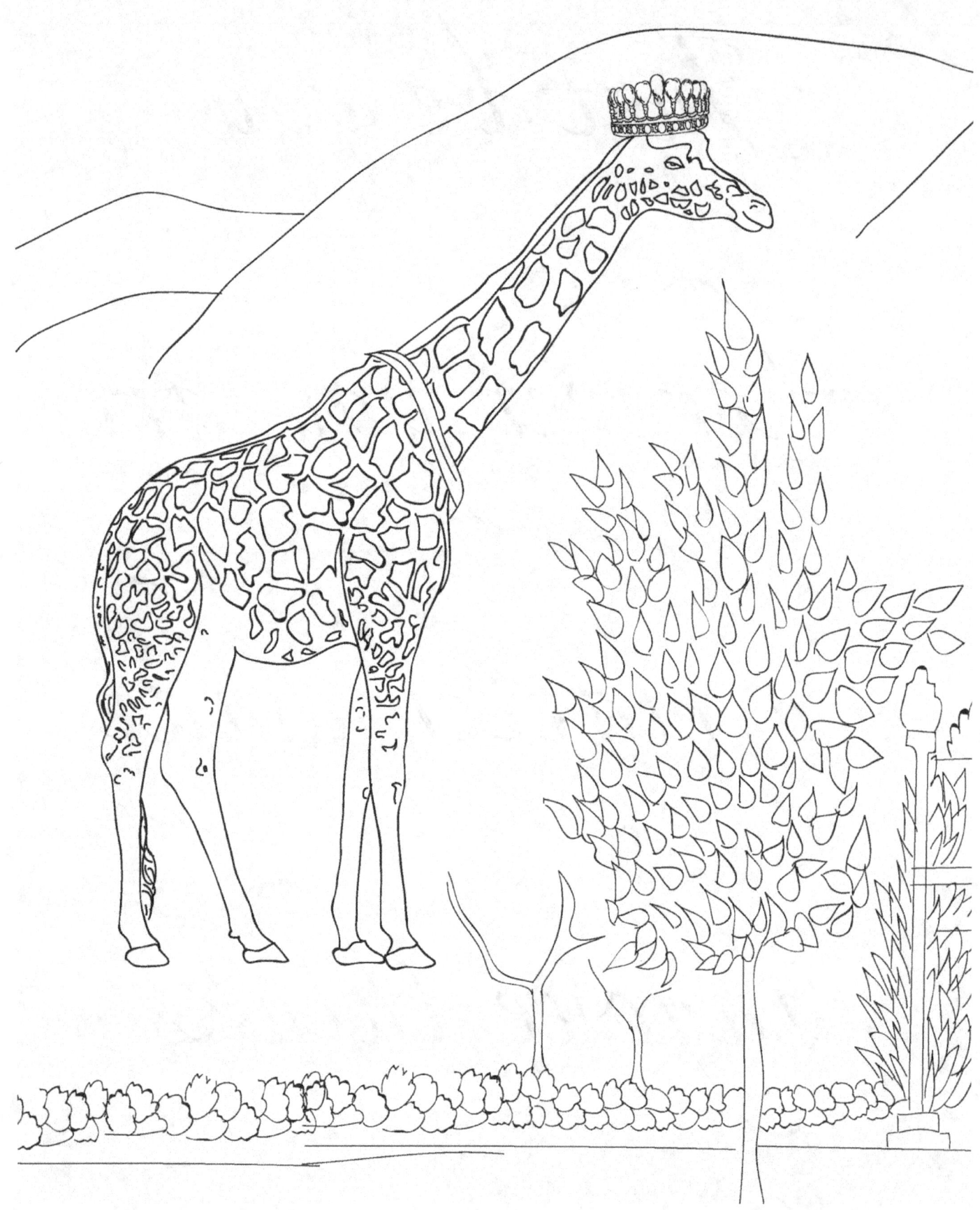

Sometimes people
can't see what you
see — that's ok
let them be

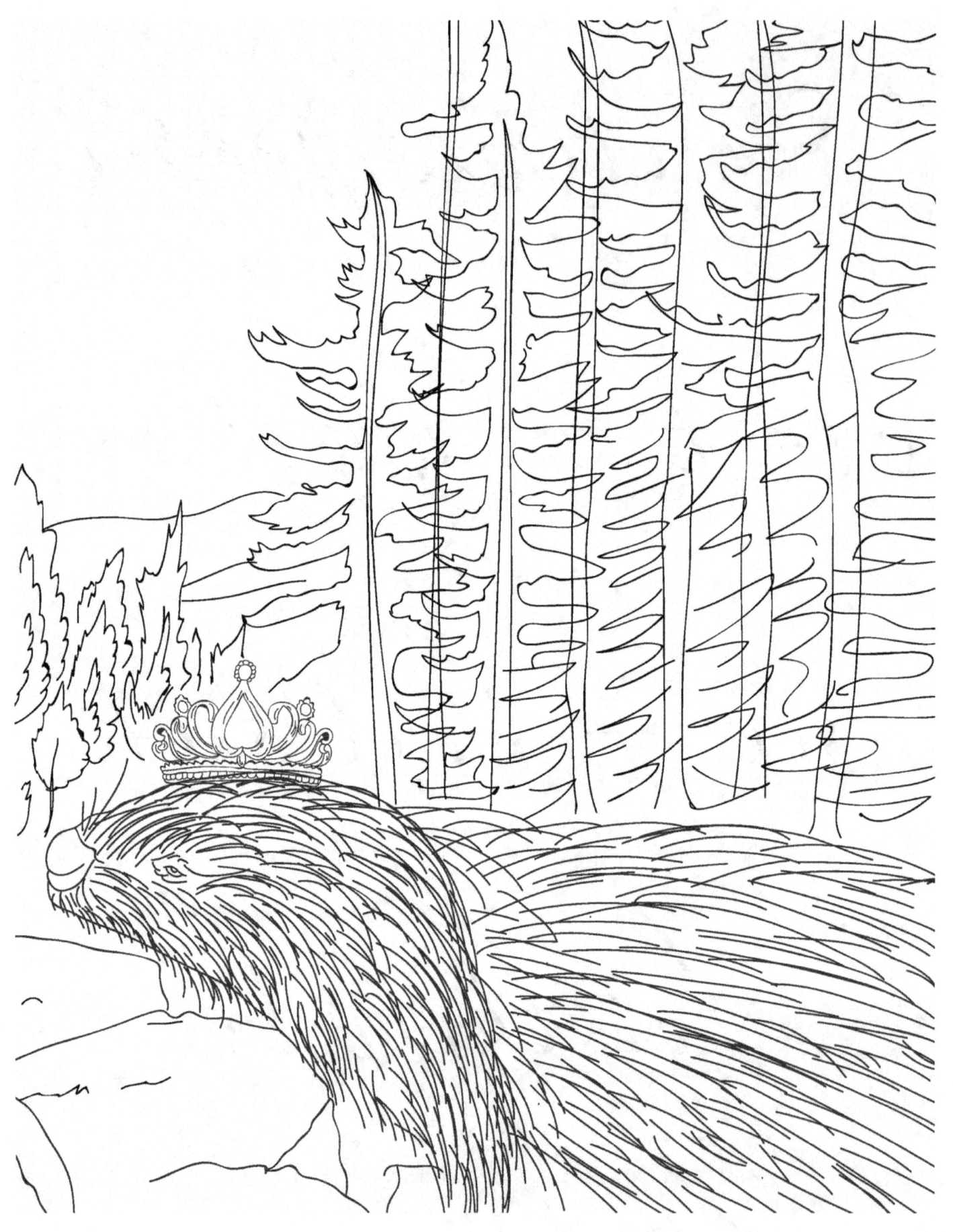

Fuzzy creatures

are the cutest

until they're

wet

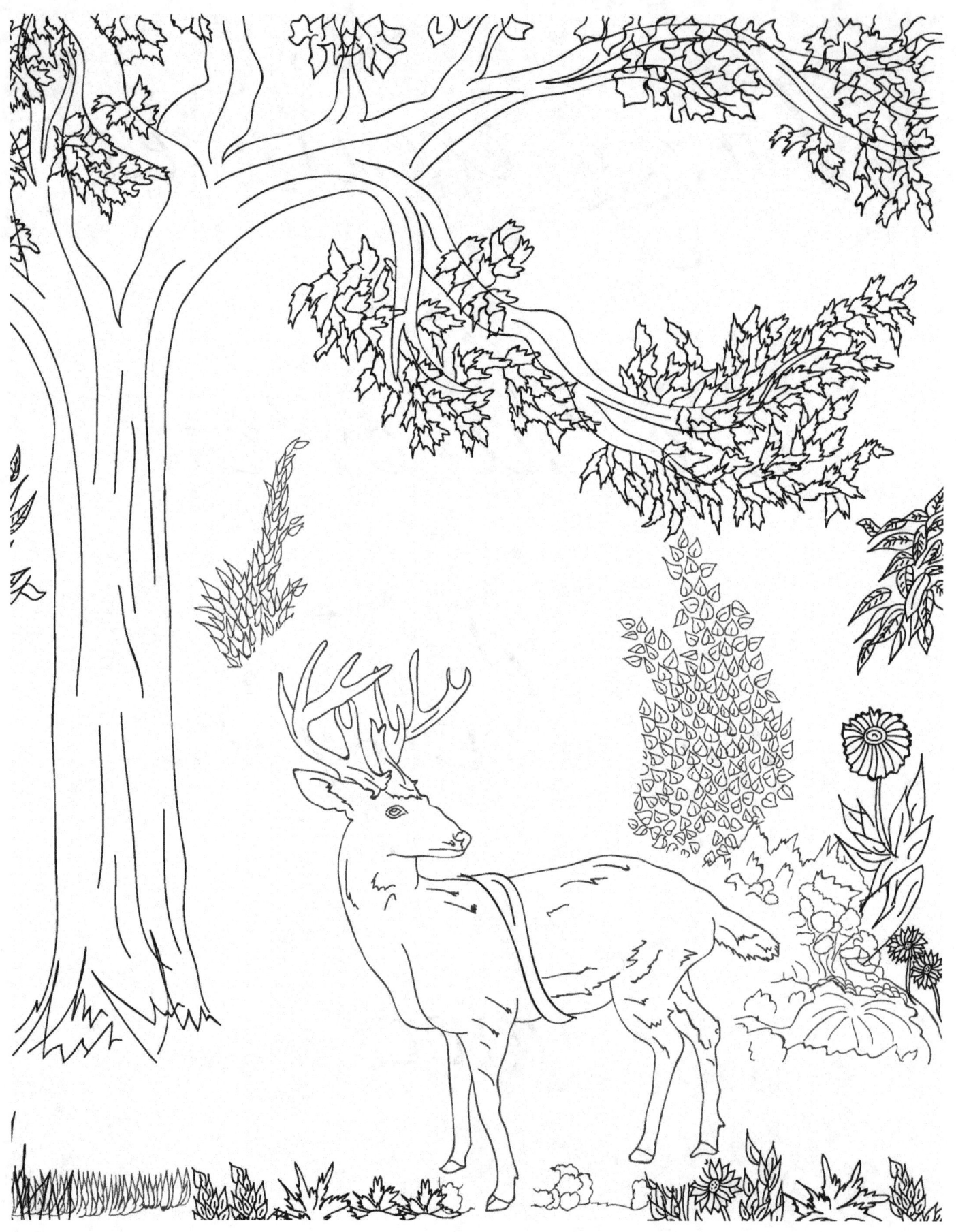

Stay alert

Someone is always

on the hunt

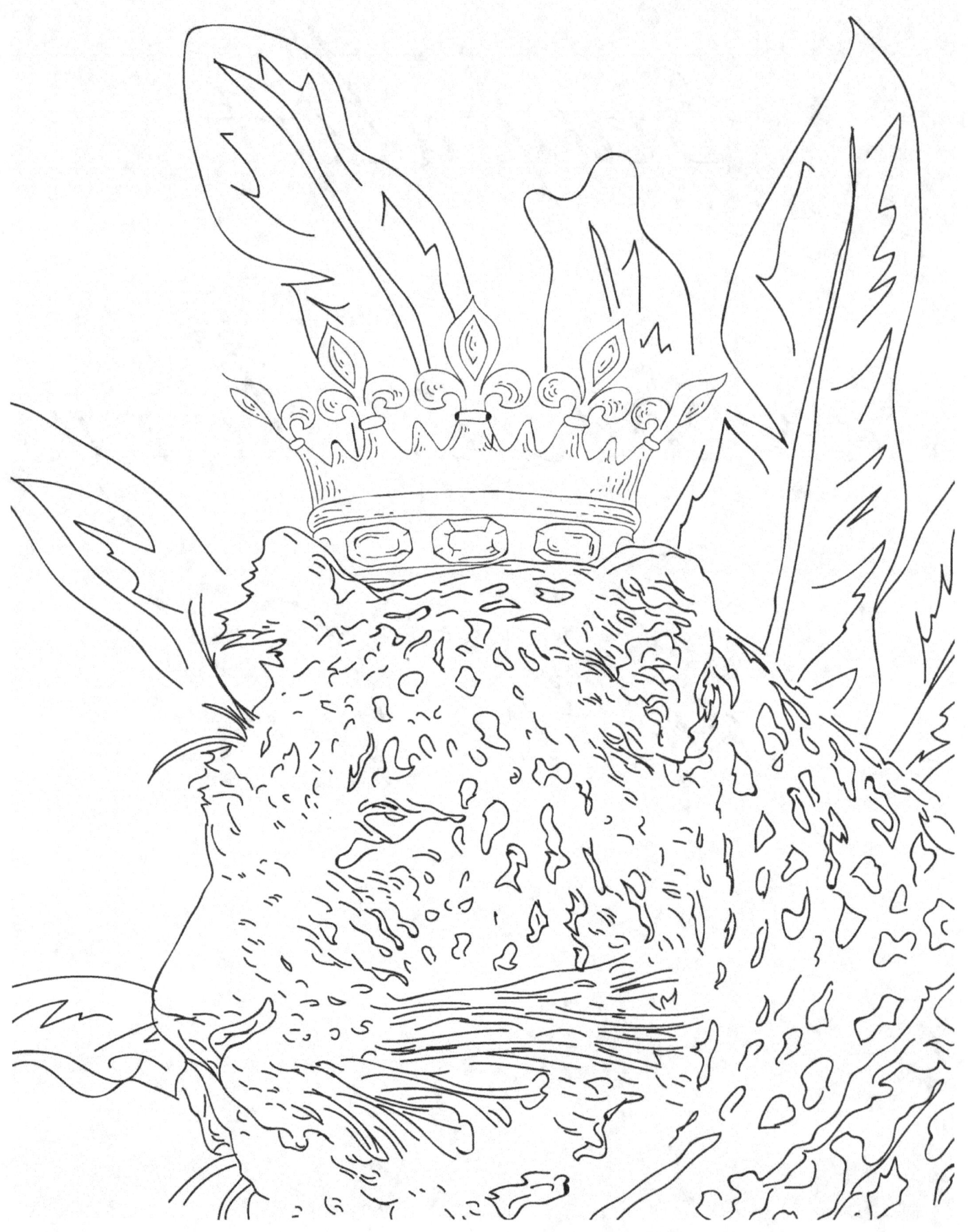

Plan to run faster

than anyone else

to get there first

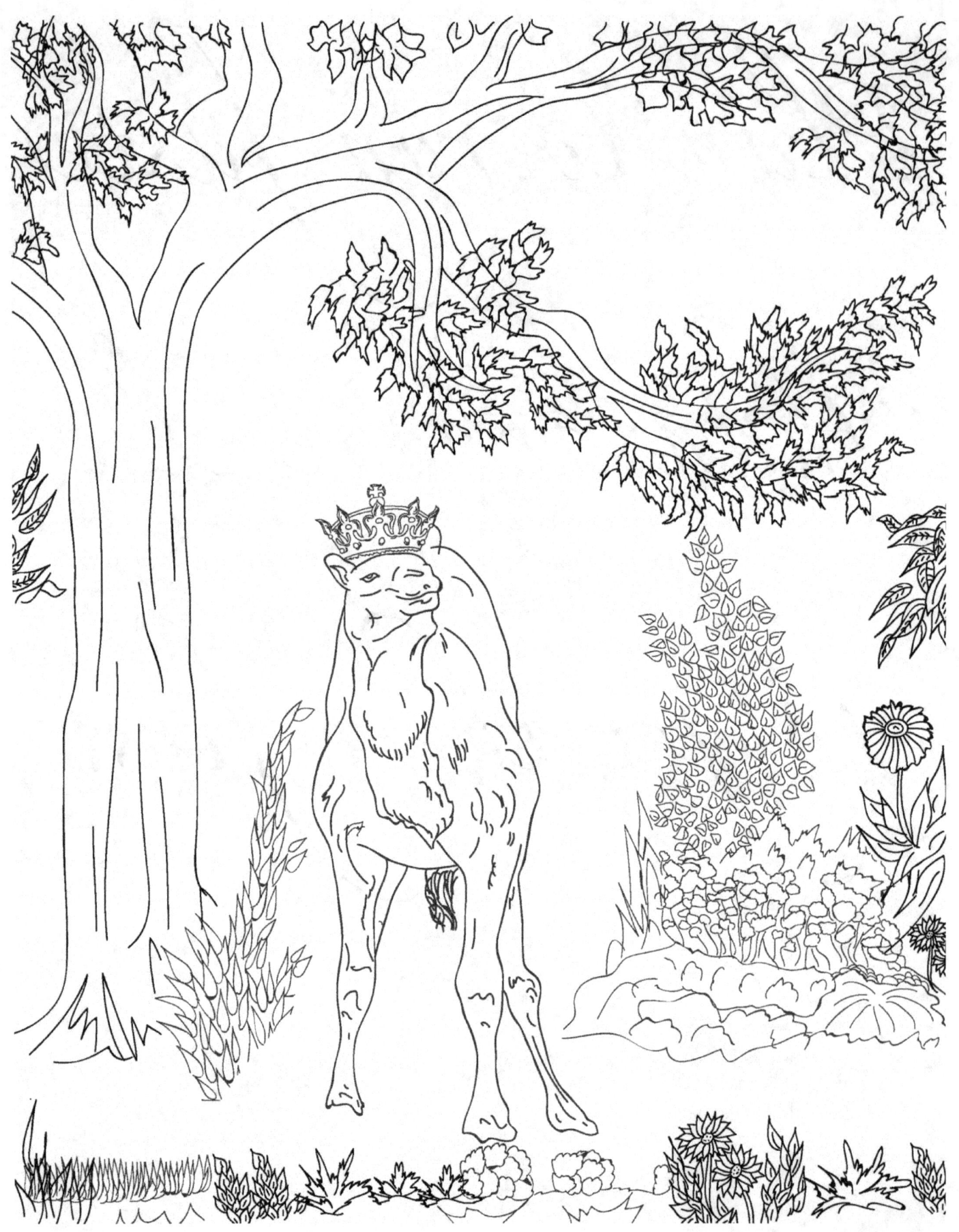

Don't be too

afraid to say

I'm not giving

rides today

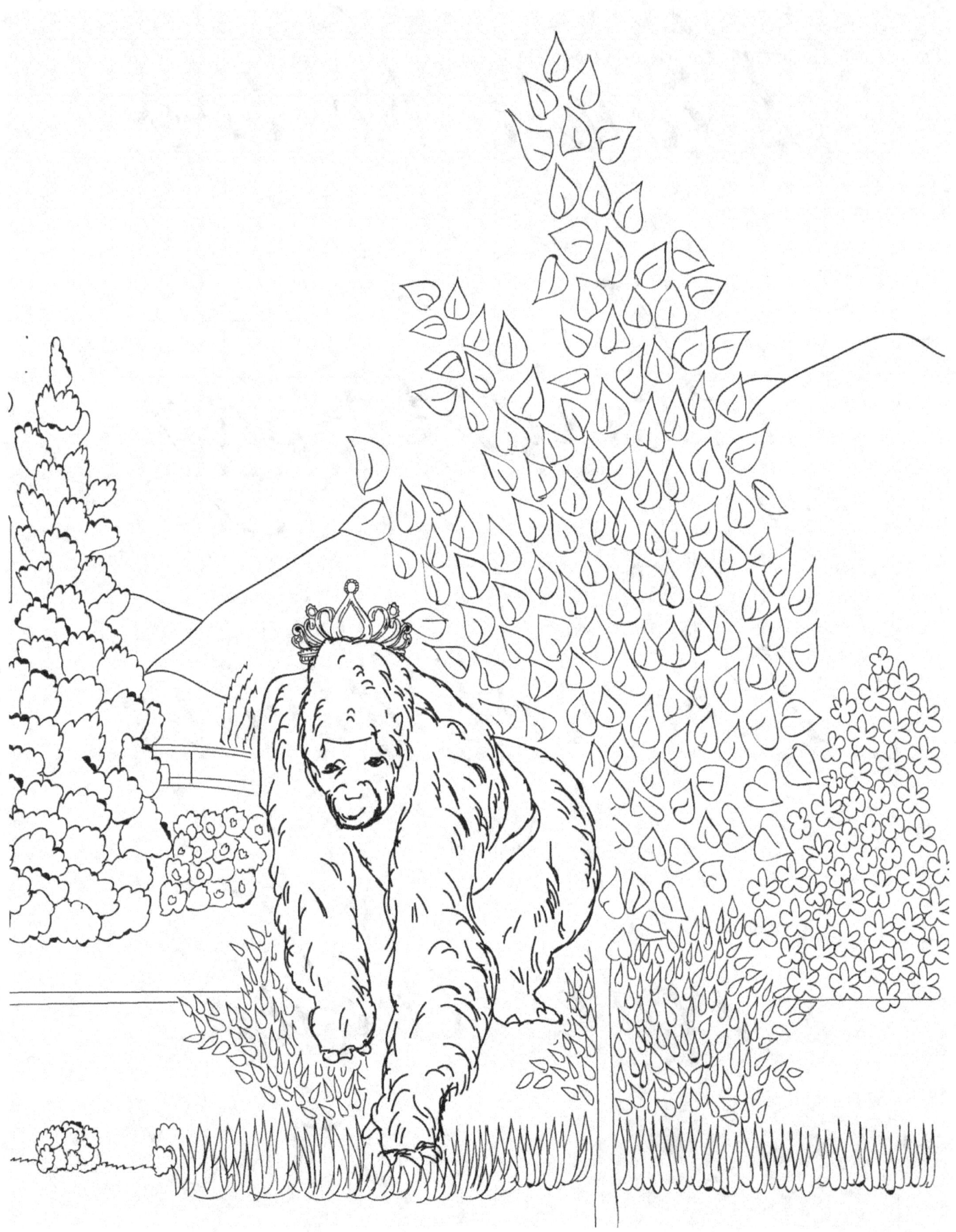

Walk slowly

and pound hard

so they hear you

coming

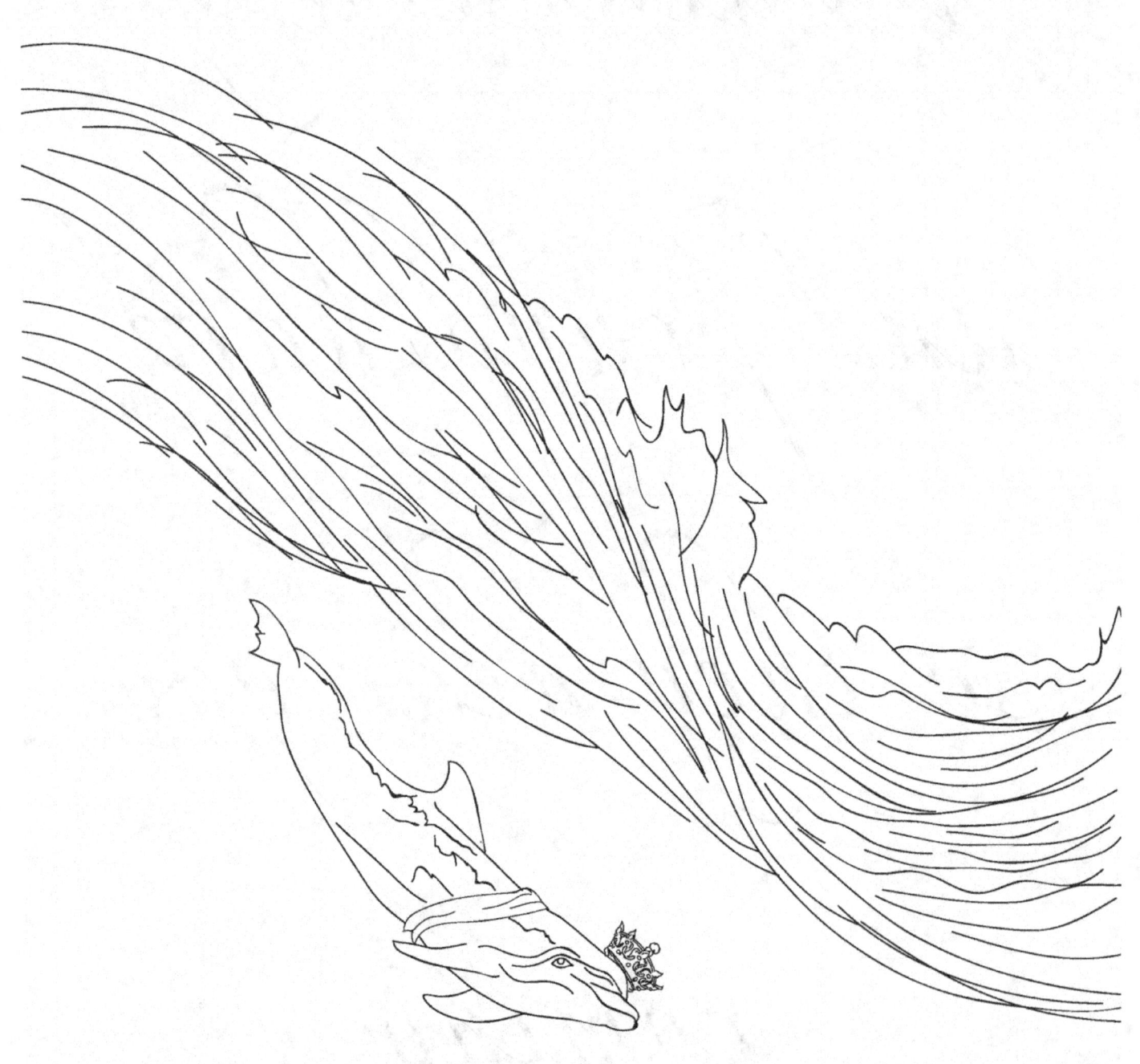

Ride

Every

Wave

- A.M.